elf Pets

An
Arctic Fox
Tradition

by
Chanda A. Bell

The
LumiStella
Company

www.lumistella.com

To all the kids who just need a dash of hope,
to Taylor, Kendyl and Murry, and a special
thanks to Russ Coddington for his tireless
work at the North Pole.
—CAB

Published by
CCA and B, LLC d/b/a The Lumistella Company
3350 Riverwood Parkway SE, Suite 300
Atlanta, GA 30339 USA - É.U. - EE.UU.

https://www.elfontheshelf.com

First Edition
11 10 9 8 7 6 5 4 3 2
Library of Congress Cataloging-in-Publication Data

Bell, Chanda A.
    Elf Pets: An Arctic Fox Tradition / written by Chanda A. Bell—1st ed. p. cm.

Summary: Elf Pets: An Arctic Fox Tradition reveals how Santa's Christmas Eve journey occurs in one night. A
wondrous arctic fox sets polar lights aglow that pause time and protect his sleigh. Thousands of fox cubs inspire
hope in children whose joy ensures "The Song of Christmas" reverberates around the world, carrying the universal
message that joy resides in the gifts of the human heart, and faith, rather than fear, raises Christmas Spirit.
—Provided by Publisher

ISBN-13: 978-0-9988109-9-7

When Christmas winds whisper gently on air,
And snow owls screech to alert polar bears,
It's time for the one who's been hidden from sight
To wake from her sleep in the frosted moonlight.

She unfurls her tail and perks up her ears,
Just like she's done for thousands of years.
Santa is calling—his voice on the wind—
He beckons to her, so she runs to her friend.

She floats over snow like a phantom on air.
All hope to glimpse her. A peek is quite rare.
Her prints can't be found. There's never a trace.
In seconds, she crosses the vast arctic space.

She reaches the mountain and pauses on top,
Looking down in the valley through icy treetops.

Her eyes become narrow. They're sharp like a hawk.

She spies St. Nick under Father Time's clock.

The clock starts to chime. It's soulful and deep—
It's almost Christmas! She lunges then leaps.
She swirls her huge tail and with all her might
Drives it to earth to spark the grand light.

Each time her tail brushes the snow,

Icy prisms take flight that cause a great glow.

The shades of green mingle. They dance in the sky,

And form Santa's route so the great sleigh can fly.

The lights flicker and bob, but wait patiently

To see the miracle of Santa flying so easily

Through air undetected without worry of time.

The lights shield and protect him; they even pause time.

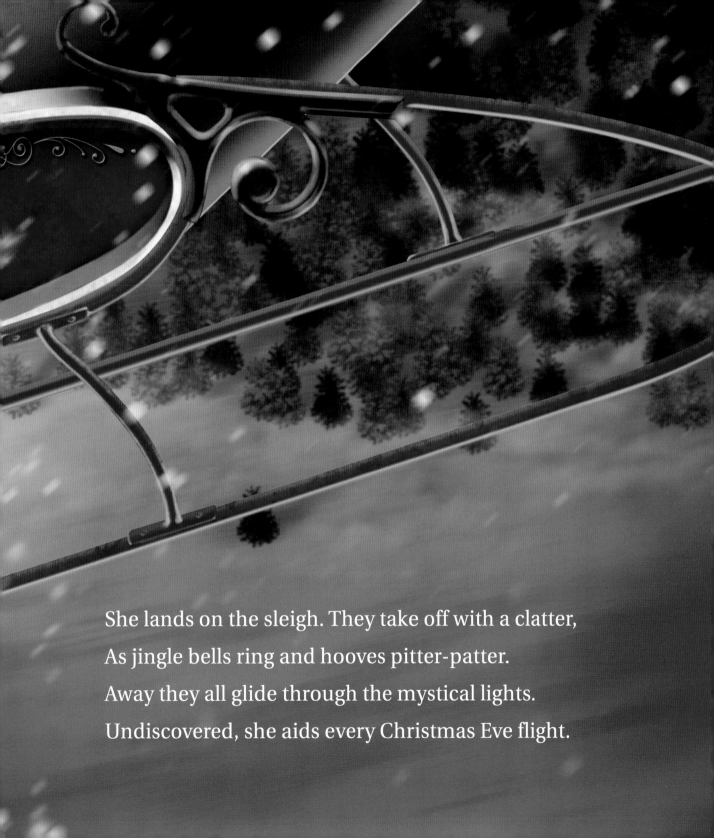

She lands on the sleigh. They take off with a clatter,

As jingle bells ring and hooves pitter-patter.

Away they all glide through the mystical lights.

Undiscovered, she aids every Christmas Eve flight.

At each little rooftop, she spins and she whirls
Her tail through the air to create snowy swirls.
She layers each home with just enough snow
For the sleigh to land with its precious cargo.

Together they work with a driven ambition,
For the simple reward of their gift-giving mission…

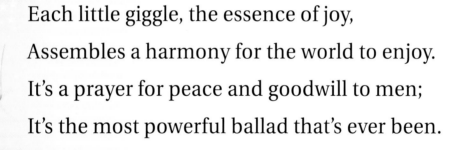

The world will rejoice as all children make

The melody of Christmas, which starts as they wake!

Each little giggle, the essence of joy,

Assembles a harmony for the world to enjoy.

It's a prayer for peace and goodwill to men;

It's the most powerful ballad that's ever been.

"It makes the lights glow even brighter you see,

Which fights against darkness—my great enemy!"

Santa notes as they all sing in utter delight,

"It's a sign to the heavens, Christmas Spirit's all right!"

The Scout Elves and Elf Pets also join in

Relieved "The Song of Christmas" is repeating again.

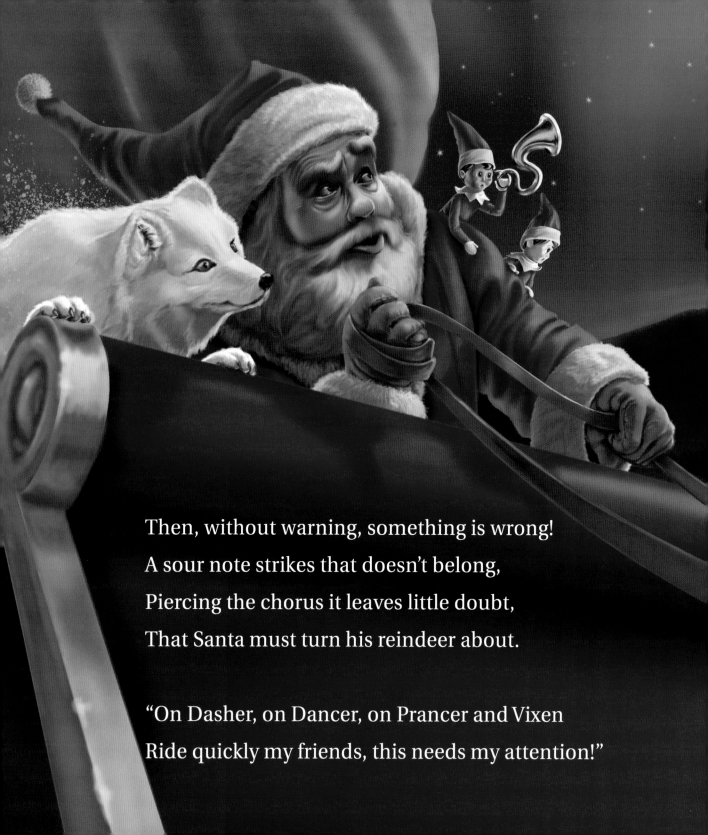

Then, without warning, something is wrong!
A sour note strikes that doesn't belong,
Piercing the chorus it leaves little doubt,
That Santa must turn his reindeer about.

"On Dasher, on Dancer, on Prancer and Vixen
Ride quickly my friends, this needs my attention!"

'Tis nearly the morning. The great veil of lights
Begins to fade with the dawn of daylight.
The magic of Christmas is starting to wane,
Yet reindeer push onward, despite heavy strain.

Then through a window at the edge of the night,

A child sits troubled even despite,

A room full of presents meant to bring glee.

The elves look to Santa, "How can this be?"

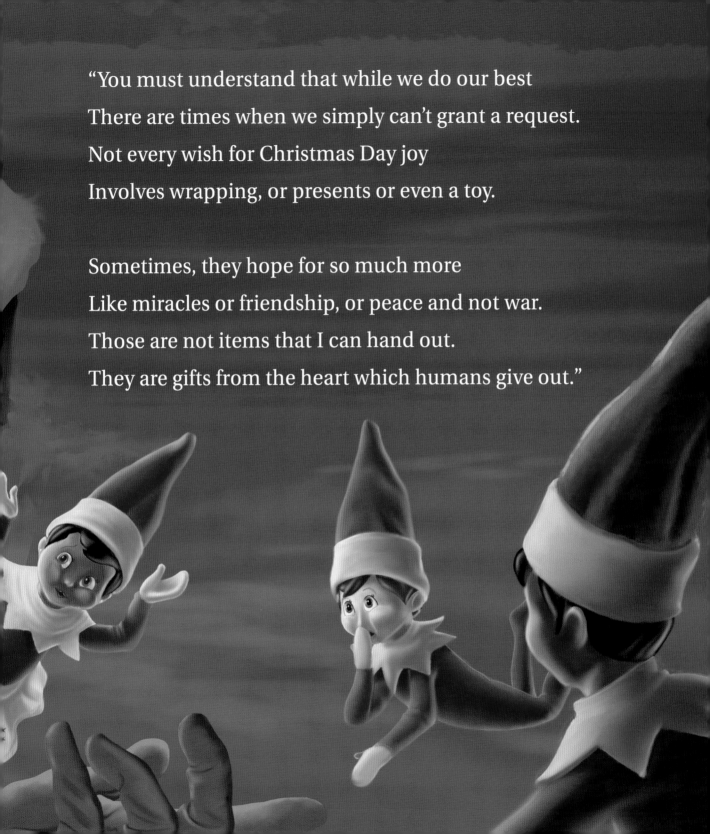

"You must understand that while we do our best
There are times when we simply can't grant a request.
Not every wish for Christmas Day joy
Involves wrapping, or presents or even a toy.

Sometimes, they hope for so much more
Like miracles or friendship, or peace and not war.
Those are not items that I can hand out.
They are gifts from the heart which humans give out."

Noorah nods, and then leaps away.

"Bong!" the clock tolls! Santa hurries the sleigh.

He waves to the fox, and with no time to spare

He pushes the sleigh up, up through the air.

The lights fade into darkness and don't leave a trace.

The clock returns to its pre-Christmas pace.

The mission is over, but the North Pole is eerie—

No poppers, balloons or ticker-tape cheering!

Santa is quiet, but oddly at ease.

He escapes to the forest—hidden by trees.

The low-spirited bunch waits without cheer,

"Will Christmas come at all this next year?"

The elves offer sadly, "Why'd the fox stay?"

Another one asks, "How can we hide the sleigh?

How can it journey through space and time

Without polar lights at Christmastime?"

"And then there's the darkness," an elf tries to convey,

" 'The Song of Christmas' could stop! We must find a way!"

Then suddenly fox cubs dart into view.

In the middle, Santa stands, holding a few.

The North Pole is elated! "But what can they do?"

Some say, "They're just pups, not even age two!"

"We can trust kids just like before,"

Santa says as cubs roll on the snow-covered floor.

"Noorah was ready! She knew that one day,

She could be the gift left by my sleigh.

We had a plan to model true love,

To offer up hope and help a child feel loved.

Each of these cubs will indeed do the same.

They'll be adopted by kids and given a name.

They'll remind kids their answers don't always come

In the way people want them, but they mustn't become

Fearful or faithless for that's the great foe

Of Christmas Spirit and all that we know.

These pups will carry our Christmas-kissed snow;

Kids shake it and swirl it, to let us all know,

When they choose faith and the will to believe;

It's the most powerful news that we can receive!

Then the night before Christmas their magical heart

Made of Christmas Spirit will do its part,

And the cubs will thrive on children's joy

And the power of hope within each girl and boy.

Swooping their tails with all of their might

Down to the ground will cause the grand light.

The sparks will assemble and once again glow
Shielding me in the heavens from dangers below.
Just like their mom, these cute cubs will make
Rooftops glitter with magic snowflakes.

Once more kids will prove, they are the reason,
'The Song of Christmas' grows stronger with each passing season!"

We welcomed our Elf Pets® Arctic Fox on

_____ , 20___.

We chose the name:

_____

We promise to choose hope
and carry the joy of Christmas
in our hearts all year long.